PORTRAIT OF A PEOPLE

A personal photographic record of the South African liberation struggle

Eli Weinberg

International Defence and Aid Fund for Southern Africa
London 1981

The International Defence and Aid Fund for Southern Africa has the following objects:–

1. To aid, defend and rehabilitate the victims of unjust legislation and oppressive and arbitrary procedures;

2. To support their families and dependants;

3. To keep the conscience of the world alive to the issues at stake.

ISBN No. 0 904759 423

Contents

Acknowledgements

ACKNOWLEDGEMENTS

I am grateful to three friends from Holland — Conny Braam, Joost Guntenaar and Willie van Exter — who persuaded me to compile this book. Joost Guntenaar also helped by putting his darkroom and studio at my disposal to prepare the prints.

The Amsterdam Municipal Arts Council very generously provided a grant to enable me to complete the task in Amsterdam.

I am indebted to the African National Congress of South Africa, to the members constituting the Congress Alliance and to the heroic people of South Africa. They are the subject of this book and their ideals, their struggles and their achievements inspired these photographs.

Finally, I thank the International Defence and Aid Fund for undertaking the publication. The Fund is in this way contributing to the recording of an important piece of history in the long human striving for emancipation.

Introduction

The photographs in this book are about the movement for freedom in South Africa. They cover key issues and events which occurred between the mid-forties and the early sixties. Some have been published before, originally in *New Age* (about which more later in this introduction), as well as in other publications issued by the African National Congress of South Africa and by various anti-apartheid organisations. I make no claim to historical or chronological completeness, but I hope that the character of both the struggle against apartheid and the people involved in the liberation movement will emerge from these pictures. In particular, I hope my photographs will show that a deep-rooted resistance movement against apartheid has always existed and continues to exist in South Africa; that this movement has well-considered directions and objectives; and that at every stage of its development it has had, and continues to have, the loyal and enthusiastic support of the majority of South Africans.

About myself. I was born in 1908 in the port of Libau on the Baltic. The years of the First World War and the October Revolution of 1917, which I experienced as a child, led me in my youth to socialism and to the working class movement. At the age of sixteen I joined a trade union and soon became deeply involved in its activities. Latvia was then an 'independent' republic with strong leanings towards the Italian model of fascism. Later the rise of Hitler in neighbouring Germany added to this tendency. In 1928, during a general strike in protest against proposed anti-trade union legislation, I had, in company with many others, my first taste of prison life. In 1929 I left Latvia and eventually landed in Cape Town on 9 December 1929. I lived in South Africa until 1976 and I consider myself a South African, although I have repeatedly been refused citizenship due to my political and trade union activities against apartheid. I joined the then legal Communist Party of South Africa in 1932 and from 1933 to 1953 was active in the trade union movement in Cape Town, Port Elizabeth and Johannesburg. With the advent of the present regime in 1948 I was 'listed' and banned from the trade unions. From 1953 I lived under a succession of banning orders. I was detained for three months during the State of Emergency in 1960, and in September 1964 I was arrested together with Bram Fischer and held in prison for seven months. At the end of a lengthy trial I was found guilty of being a member of the Central Committee of the underground South African Communist Party and sentenced to five years' imprisonment. On being released in April 1970 I was again served with banning orders, which restricted me to my house apart from my daily report to the police station. In 1976, during the Soweto upheavals, I left South Africa illegally on instructions of the African National Congress, and I now live in Dar es Salaam, where the Government of Tanzania has given me political asylum.

My interest in photography dates back to about 1926, when I assisted part-time in a photographic studio belonging to a friend. During my first months in South Africa I worked as a professional photographer, and during my following 20 years of work in the trade unions I continued to take a serious interest in photography, exhibiting and publishing often. After I was banned from the trade unions, despite restrictions, imprisonment and house-arrest, I proceeded to build up a successful and extensive practice with my own studio.

I contributed often to exhibitions and salons. Shortly before my arrest in 1964 I was awarded the silver medal at a colour slide exhibition at the New York World Fair. I was under the usual banning order at the time and the Johannesburg *Sunday Express* reported on 17 May 1964:

'A Johannesburg photographer won a silver medal at the New York World Fair. But, as a listed communist banned from attending gatherings, he was unable to attend the presentation ceremony in Johannesburg on Friday.

The photographer is Mr. Eli Weinberg, of Plantation Road, Gardens.

Mr. Weinberg won the medal and a cheque for 100 dollars with a colour slide of a group of Basuto women. The photograph was taken in the Maluti mountains two years ago.

The slide was one of 150,000 entries from 58 countries submitted to the New York World Fair.

Only 300 were selected for exhibition, and Mr. Weinberg was included among the prize winners.

At the official presentation, Mr. J. J. Wessels, President of the Institute of Professional Photographers, accepted the medal for Mr. Weinberg.'

In my precipate flight from South Africa I was unable to take with me my collection of negatives built up over the years. When I subsequently tried to recover them, there occurred one of those tragedies which are the inevitable by-product of an active political life. In a sad set of circumstances the bulk of my collection was lost or destroyed and I managed to recover only a small percentage of the total. Of this, the photographs in this book are a selection.

Most of these pictures were done on assignments for *New Age,* an independent, progressive weekly which supported the African National Congress. This work was a source of great pleasure and inspiration to me and I am grateful for the opportunities of relief from the routine of commercial photography which *New Age* afforded me. Here I must mention Ruth First, an editor of *New Age*, under whose direction I carried out many interesting assignments. I also helped to train other photographers for *New Age*, as my restrictions often prevented me from undertaking assignments. Amongst my most successful students was Joe Gqabi, a conscientious, dedicated and courageous newspaper man. I greatly cherish the intimate friendship which developed between us as a result of our work together. Joe has since served twelve years on Robben Island, was put under house-arrest after his release from prison, and then rearrested and held awaiting trial for some sixteen months, finally to be acquitted in the trial of 'The Pretoria Twelve'. His acquittal undoubtedly owed much to the tremendous waves of protest which were generated by anti-apartheid forces in every part of the world.

As the main credit for the photographs in this book is due to *New Age*, it is appropriate to tell its story here. This weekly newspaper was the successor to the *Guardian*, an anti-fascist paper started in 1937 by a group of enthusiasts who understood the need for a periodical which would take an effective stand against racialism in South Africa—an institutionalised racialism which at that time was being inflamed by the local development of groups taking their ideals from the Fascist and Nazi regimes then nearing the height of their power in Europe. (Some of the present rulers of South Africa were to be found in the ranks of those groups.) It required a great deal of courage to venture out with a new paper at this time, not least because there was never any hope of financial support from advertisers.

Nevertheless, the *Guardian* soon won the support of working people in every part of the country; often its circulation reached between 40,000 and 50,000 per week, a prodigious achievement in a country where illiteracy is rife and poverty is widespread. When the present regime came to power it decided to ban the *Guardian* and a countrywide 'Defend the *Guardian*' campaign developed.

Joe Gqabi in his family circle shortly after his release from Robben Island in 1975.

7

The *Guardian* was banned in 1952, but was followed by another, similar newspaper, and then when that was banned in turn, by yet another, and again another; with foresight the names of a line of successors had already been registered. Thus the *Guardian* was followed by *People's World, Advance*, the *Clarion*, and *New Age*. After the closing down of *New Age* on 30 November 1962, *Spark* survived for four months, after which every contributor and worker on the paper was prohibited from writing or preparing material for publication. Thus ended a quarter of a century of the only newspaper in South Africa to have expressed the interests of the majority. In 1977, when *The World*, a black orientated paper of the Argus group of companies, became outspoken on such questions as Bantu Education and the murder of children in the streets of Soweto, it suffered the same fate as the *Guardian*, and *New Age*. In South Africa the press has no freedom to reveal the truth about apartheid.

A 'Defend the *Guardian*' meeting in Johannesburg.

I will shortly be seventy years old,* and in the biblical tradition of 'three score years and ten' it would seem that I have 'had it'. But I am sustained by the hope that I may yet return to a free South Africa. The movement for liberation has taken great strides in recent years.

I was among many others who, during the night of 16 December, 1961, went out to paste up and distribute the announcement that a military wing of the African National Congress, *Umkhonto we Sizwe*, the Spear of the Nation, had been formed. Sadly, I am too old to record the exploits of our brave fighters on film, but I know that many young people will come to do this, and their work will inspire us to further efforts.

The flood of young people into our ranks in search of knowledge and training, particularly in search of political education, is our guarantee that the slogan of the ANC—*Amandla Ngawethu, Matla Ke a Rona*—Power to the People—will be realised. I hope that, by referring to our past, this book will in a small way also help to inspire others in the struggle for this future.

*Written in 1978

Housing

Shanty towns and 'housing schemes'

During the Second World War and immediately after, industrial expansion in South Africa drew thousands of workers from the impoverished countryside into the cities. Employers welcomed this flow and the government pushed it along by increased taxes of all kinds, yet nobody cared about providing houses for the growing population

'Housing' in shanty towns.

in the cities. All kinds of shanty towns grew up. It was a dismal scene. The shanty towns had no water and no proper sanitation and they became a major health hazard.

Only when disease threatened to spread to the affluent white areas, were some halfhearted measures taken to build what were called homes. For instance, in and around what is now Soweto, rows of one-roomed shacks were erected without

Sometimes, there is only one water tap per street.

Orlando power station provides power for the needs of the whites. It is only one kilometer from Soweto, but there are no street lights in Soweto and apart from a handful of houses occupied by wealthy Africans there is no electricity in the houses.

internal partitions, without floors, without ceilings—the tenants had to provide the internal amenities at their own expense in addition to paying frequently rising rentals.

As soon as such official 'housing schemes' were established they were brought under the control of a white superintendent and his staff of clerks and policemen. Barbed wire fences were erected with gates which were, and are, guarded against unauthorised 'trespassers'. Permits are needed to enter such townships. Often these permits are only obtainable at the office of the superintendent inside the township, so that permit seekers may even be arrested on the way to getting one. Casual visitors need permits; there are tenants' permits and lodgers' permits. Frequent raids are carried out during the night to check on 'illegal' residents and both tenants and lodgers are liable to arrest, heavy fines, and even imprisonment, for transgressions.

The spontaneous erection of shanty towns continues in every part of the country, because the government does not provide adequate housing, yet at the same time persists in carrying out large scale and numerous removals of blacks from so-called 'black spots' to remote desolate areas. Meanwhile, tens of thousands are on the waiting list for a house in Soweto, and tens of thousands live there 'illegally'.

Some employers provide 'free' housing for their migrant labourers. Views of a typical 'compound'.

17

Labour

The cheap labour system

The real purpose of apartheid has been stated frankly by white South African states-
men. Dr. H. F. Verwoerd, usually credited with being the 'architect' of apartheid
(although he merely formalised an already well established system), said:

> 'there is no place for the black man in the white economy other than in certain
> forms of labour . . .'

Migrant workers, contracted to work in the gold mines, arrive in Johannesburg with their miserable
belongings of sleeping mats and working clothes, to be allocated to different mines.

A less sophisticated member of his party, a Mr. Froneman, equated Africans to 'asses and oxen', who were useful for pulling the white man's ploughs and carts.

Basically, the purpose of apartheid is to ensure a plentiful supply of cheap labour for the white dominated economy. An intricate network of laws and institutions has been evolved, which dominates the lives of the blacks from the cradle to the grave, to ensure that the phenomenal rates of profit available to the South African white

Miners at the 'face'.

Conditions in a flour mill.

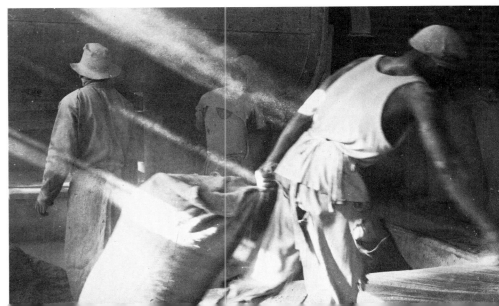

Workers in the engineering industry.

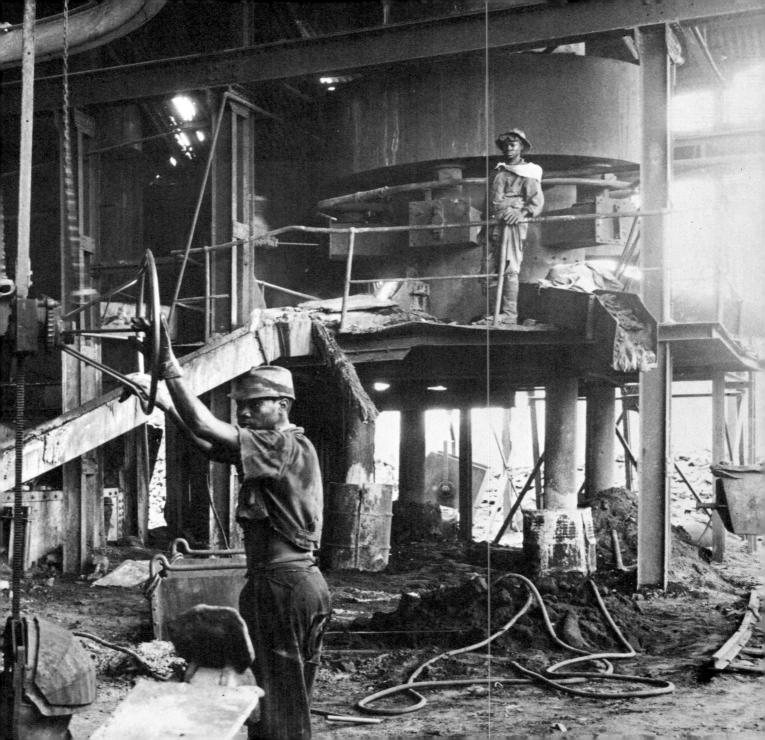

Rest room facilities at places of work are inadequate. Workers prefer to spend their lunch hour in the street.

'Coffee stalls' outside factories sell cheap lunches to the workers, but the authorities disapprove of this kind of black private enterprise and the vendors are hounded by the police and inspectors under all kinds of pretexts.

economy and its overseas partners should be maintained and, if possible, perpetuated for all time.

Workers, whether migrant labourers recruited from the country for limited periods or third and fourth generation urban workers, are all nothing more than 'units' to be shifted around at will and at the discretion of unscrupulous employers, whose only concern is to get rich quickly. Work and leisure facilities are kept to a minimum and if as a result the worker's health is affected and his ability to produce profits is reduced, he becomes 'redundant' and can be sent to some 'homeland' through the pipeline of apartheid, there to finish his days in misery and grinding poverty.

Anxiety and frustration. If you don't get a job within 72 hours, or if your pass is not in order, you may be 'endorsed out' of the urban area and forcibly sent back to a Bantustan, where you may have never been before, where you know nobody and where there is no work, no food, and perhaps no shelter.

Control of labour: the Pass Laws

Every Adult African over the age of sixteen must carry a 'pass' and must be able to produce it on demand at any time of day or night. The pass is obtained at so called 'Pass Offices', where applicants are carefully screened by a computerised index. Each morning hundreds of people in need of various documents or 'endorsements' to documents line up outside these pass offices, which also deal with work seekers. The queues begin to form early in the morning before sunrise, but many do not manage to get processed during the day and return again the next morning.

Outside a Pass Office.

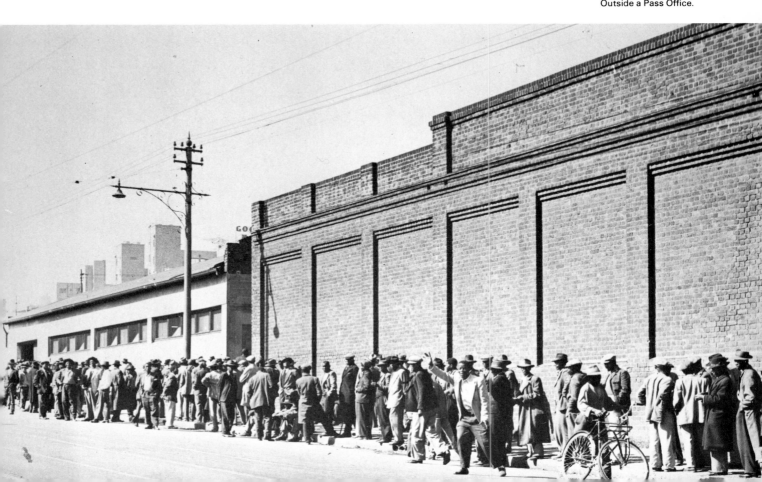

Johannesburg's Labour Bureau in Albert Street.

Waiting, for hours, to be processed for work and passes.

Inside a Pass Office.

Pass raids are a daily feature in the lives of Africans. They take place at arbitrary times, at bus stops, railway stations, factory gates or in the dead of night during house-to-house searches.

The old man is probably three times the age of the constable, but the latter will refer to him as 'boy'.

Even if the pass is in order, the constable must display his superiority as a white man. He humiliates the black man by a completely unnecessary examination of his personal belongings.

Pass checks.

This woman, whose pass was not in order, pleaded that she had small children at home. She is detained.

Another woman who intervenes on her behalf is also arrested.

As she resists, re-inforcement is called.

Several burly policemen bundle the women into the pick-up van.

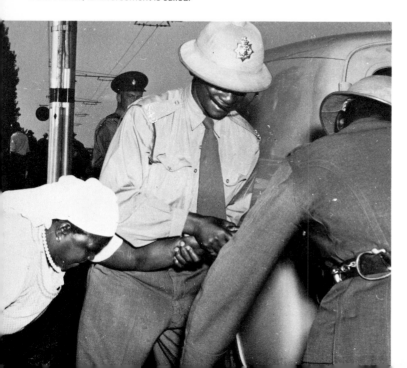

Waiting to be transported.

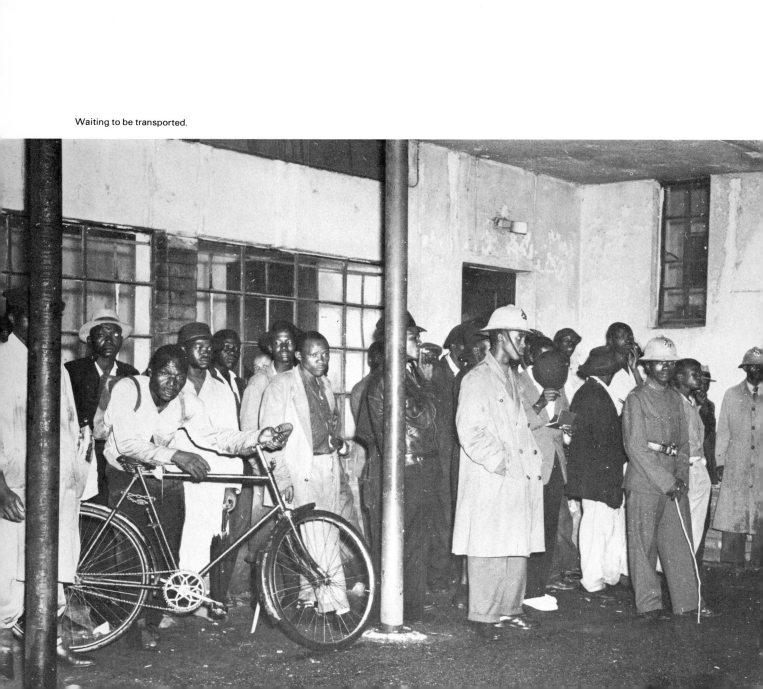

Off to jail.

Those found without passes or with faulty documents are detained, handcuffed and assembled to be loaded into waiting vehicles, which travel around until they are full and then proceed to various police stations. There the prisoners are locked up in cells until the following morning, when they will appear before a Bantu Commissioner acting as a magistrate. These special courts dispose of, on average, between 300 and 400 cases during a morning session, an average of one minute per case. Eleven million people served prison sentences for pass offences between 1948 and 1973. As the average black population during this period was about 16 million, it can be said that there is hardly a black man or woman who has not at one time or another gone to jail.

Convicted pass offenders at work.

Once in jail for a pass offence, the prisoner is sent to work, sometimes for a white farmer in a distant rural area, sometimes in the garden of a government official. *New Age* successfully exposed a racket, whereby pass offenders were 'sold' by pass officials in Alexandra, Johannesburg, to waiting farmers.

Gert Sibande, an ANC organiser in the Eastern Transvaal, known as the 'Lion of the East', helped in a legal action which resulted in liberating the men in the next photograph.

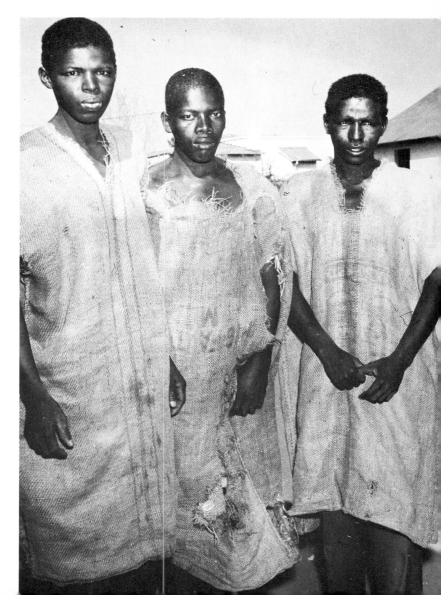

These men were missed by their families for weeks. They were found in the Eastern Transvaal and brought back, still dressed in the sacks issued to them as working clothes.

Trade Unionism

The Unions—divided and ruled by Apartheid

Like everything else in South Africa, the trade union movement is bedevilled by colour and race issues. There are separate organisations for White, Coloured, Indian and African workers. White, Coloured, and Indian trade unions enjoy a measure of 'recognition' and collective bargaining under the Industrial Conciliation Act, though at the price of strict government control and loss of independence. African workers have been excluded from the Industrial Conciliation Act and their unions not recognised. Coloured and Indian workers, who may be members of 'mixed' trade unions, may not serve on their Executive Committees, which must be white.

The defenders of the system (including some multinational companies who invest in South Africa) argue that 'Africans are not ripe for trade unionism'. This is belied by the history of African trade unionism. The Industrial and Commercial Workers' Union (ICU), formed in 1918/19 survived ten years of bitter opposition and repression and at its peak had a membership of over 100,000. Some African trade unions formed in 1927, such as the Laundry Workers' Union, still operate successfully today, having survived persecution of their members as well as lack of recognition. More than sixty years of active, virile trade union experience has therefore fitted the African workers superbly not only for managing their organisations, but for using their strength achieved through unity in many effective actions, such as the heroic strike of 60,000 members of the African Mine Workers' Union in August 1946, the stay-at-homes in 1958 and 1961, the wave of strikes in 1973 and 1974 and the effective strike actions throughout the country in 1976. In these actions many strikers were killed by the police. They were all trade union actions and proved the ability of the African workers to organise.

But this is precisely the reason why employers and the government alike prefer all kinds of substitutes for trade unionism. So called 'works committees' and 'liason committees' have been rejected by the African workers, because they are invariably under the control of the employers and of the hated apartheid authorities.

J. B. Marks, President of the African Mine Workers' Union, 1941-1949.

A group of trade unionists in Cape Town in about 1934. I am in
the middle of the front row.

Strike of white building workers in 1948. Their Secretary, Piet Huyzer (fourth from left) was later banned from the trade unions.

Officials of the African Clothing Workers' Union (about 1951). Veteran trade unionist Gana Makabeni (second from right) founded the Union in 1928. On his left is Viola Hashe, who later was Vice President of the South African Congress of Trade Unions. On the extreme left is Bertha Mashaba, an active member of the Federation of South African women.

The 1954 Executive Committee of the African Laundry Workers' Union, formed in 1927. In the middle back row is John Gaetsewe, the present Secretary General of the South African Congress of Trade Unions.

Isaac Mamakwe, banned Secretary of the Furniture, Mattress and Bedding Workers' Union. The leaflet in front of him, issued in 1954, says: 'The life of the Trade Union Movement is at stake.'

Executive Committee of the South African Railway and Harbour Workers' Union. In the second row on the left is Lawrence Ndzanga, Secretary of the Union, banned and detained for long periods without trial and finally murdered during police interrogation in 1976.

A trade union meeting at a factory. The management prevented some of the workers from leaving the premises, so they listened to the organisers from behind the barbed wire fence. Later the security police questioned the workers. Employers frequently bring in the police when workers try to organise.

Officials of the multi-racial Food and Canning Workers' Union (about 1952). Left to right: Betty du Toit, Oscar Mphetha, Ray Alexander (Ray Simons), Maria Williams and David Jantjies. The Union still carries on today, although its main officials are banned.

Milling workers on strike. These are the same workers whose conditions are depicted on page 23. Strikes of African workers were illegal under almost any circumstances. This strike was broken after several weeks by the employers and the Government Labour Department, who imported scab labour from a Bantustan.

A general meeting of Textile Workers in the Trades Hall, Johannesburg, decides on strike action if their demands are not met by the employers. (The portrait on the wall behind the officials is of Keir Hardie, a British socialist, who visited South Africa early in the century and prophesied that the workers would win a socialist commonwealth in South Africa).

The first trade unionist to be banned under the notorious Suppression of Communism Act, was E. S. (Solly) Sachs, Secretary of the Garment Workers' Union. This led to a series of demonstrations by the members of the Union, but Sachs was eventually forced to go into exile and died in London in 1975.

The Credentials Committee at a Trades and Labour Council Conference. The problem was how to keep out the blacks.

TUCSA officials: Left to right: Steve Scheepers (one of the Presidents), Dr. B. Serebro (Medical Officer), an unidentified official and Tom Murray (first President of TUCSA).

An all-white Executive Committee at all times.

These men objected to black membership. Second from left is Arthur Grobbelaar, General Secretary of TUCSA. The flashily dressed gentleman on the right is George McCormick, a rabid racialist, who was rewarded for his apartheid attitude with a life-time appointment to a high government board.

Leslie Massina, first General Secretary of SACTU who was banned, and died in exile in Swaziland.

Foundation conference of the South African Congress of Trade Unions, 5 March 1955.

The emergence of the South African Congress of Trade Unions (SACTU)

Until 1954 the main trade union co-ordinating body was the South African Trades and Labour Council and its constitution was open to membership of African trade unions. However, African trade unionists preferred to organise in the Council of Non-European Trade Unions, because they rightly resented the fact that the whites failed to elect any black members to the National Executive Committee. Some white trade unionists fought against white racism in the SATLC for many years, but were eventually defeated by the reactionary leaders, who demanded the exclusion of the African workers. As the reactionaries could not muster the two-thirds majority necessary to change the constitution, they dissolved the South African Trades and Labour Council in 1954 by a simple majority and immediately proceeded to form a new body, the present Trade Union Council of South Africa (TUCSA), which barred Africans from membership in line with the government's apartheid policies. This racial division was assisted by the fact that the government effectively removed the progressive influences, by banning some fifty trade union leaders.

The reaction of African trade unions to this betrayal of working class principles was prompt and characteristic. On 5 and 6 March 1955 a conference in Johannesburg attended by delegates from thirty-four trade unions, representing 42,000 members (including representatives of the Council of Non-European Trade Unions) formed the South African Congress of Trade Unions (SACTU) and adopted a constitution with a declaration of principles, which planted the new body firmly in the tradition of true trade unionism.

Annual Conference of SACTU, March, 1956

SACTU—DECLARATION OF PRINCIPLES

History has shown that unorganised workers are unable to improve their wages and conditions of employment on a lasting basis. Only where workers have organised in effective trade unions have they been able to improve their lot, raise their standard of living and generally protect themselves and their families against the insecurities of life.

The whole experience of the Trade Union Movement the world over has, furthermore, established the fact that the Movement can only progress on the basis of unity and in the spirit of brotherhood and the solidarity of all workers. Trade unions must unreservedly reject any attempts to sow disunity among the workers, on the basis of colour or nationality, or any other basis.

Just as the individual worker or any group of workers are unable to improve their lot without organising into a trade union, so is the individual trade union powerless unless there is in existence a co-ordinating body of trade unions which unites the efforts of all workers. For such a trade union federation to be successful, it must be able to speak on behalf of all workers, irrespective of race or colour, nationality or sex.

The future of the people of South Africa is in the hands of its workers. Only the working class in alliance with other progressive minded sections of the community, can build a happy life for all South Africans, a life free from unemployment, insecurity and poverty, free from racial hatred and oppression, a life of vast opportunities for all people.

But the working class can only succeed in this great and noble endeavour if it itself is united and strong, if it is conscious of its inspiring responsibility. The workers of South Africa need a united trade union movement in which all sections of the working class can play their part unhindered by prejudice or racial discrimination. Only such a truly united movement can serve effectively the interests of the workers, both the immediate interests of higher wages and better conditions of life and work as well as the ultimate objective of complete emancipation for which our forefathers have fought.

We firmly declare that the interests of all workers are alike, whether they be European or non-European, African, Coloured, Indian, English, Afrikaans or Jewish. We resolve that this co-ordinating body of trade unions shall strive to unite all workers in its ranks, without discrimination, and without prejudice. We resolve that this body shall determinedly seek to further and protect the interest of all workers, and that its guiding motto shall be the univeral slogan of working class solidarity:

'An injury to one is an injury to all'.

Annual Conference of SACTU, 18 March 1958. I was banned from trade union activities and from attending gatherings. The delegates assembled in a secluded court-yard and I avoided contact with them by appearing at a second floor window and quickly taking this shot.

SACTU has since then led many struggles commencing with a highly successful campaign for a national minimum wage of £1 per day. Affiliates and individual activists of SACTU have continued through the years to defend the interests of the workers and to strive for unity in the labour movement. The government reaction has been typical. Without banning SACTU outright (the ILO would have frowned on inter-ference with the workers' right to organise), repressive measures were taken against every known SACTU activist. All members of its National Executive Committee are banned. Some were banished to distant rural areas, many were detained, imprisoned, and tortured, and some died at the hands of the security police. At one stage the head office of SACTU in Johannesburg practically came to a standstill and the only person left was the typist, nineteen-year-old Miriam Sithole. As she continued to keep the office open, she too was served with a five-year banning order.

Miriam Sithole—five years house-arrest at the age of nineteen. She was detained in 1976 and held without trial for eight months.

Despite this, SACTU is still very much alive, although its activities in South Africa are largely clandestine, and new forms of organisation have had to be devised. Recently SACTU served a series of demands on the employers in South Africa, including a minimum national wage of R50 per week, and these demands have met with the enthusiastic support of the workers. SACTU's newspaper, *Workers' Unity,* which first appeared in April 1955, is circulating widely despite the fact that the South African government has banned it.

The last public conference of SACTU was held on 9 October 1960. Viola Hashe presided (she was banned after that). On the left is Don Mateman, who was also banned shortly after this conference.

Women

In the forefront of the struggle

Women have played an active part in the liberation movement; the ANC Women's League standing in the forefront in defence of women's rights in particular and the struggle for freedom in general. Some women have become leading personalities in the political life of the African people. Lilian Ngoyi, former National President of the ANC Women's League, is one example. She lived in Soweto under severe restrictions until her death in March 1980.

Lilian Ngoyi.

Women are not safe from police brutality.

Madonna and Child.

ANC Women's League members in a demonstration.

In April 1954 the Federation of South African Women came into being as a multi-racial body in support of the Congress Alliance. Ray Alexander was its first National Secretary, followed by Helen Joseph, and its first National President was Ida Mntwana, a charismatic and highly popular fighter from the western areas of Johannesburg. Later, Lilian Ngoyi was elected President.

Foundation conference of the Federation of South African Women, April 1954. Reading the address is Ray Alexander, veteran trade unionist, now living in exile in Lusaka.

A fiery Florence Matomela from the Eastern Province is listened to with approval by the delegates.

Ida Mntwana addressing the conference.

A delegation from the Transkei and from the Eastern Province.

These young girls were present at the foundation conference of the Federation. The little girl on the left is a link between the past and the present. She is Sheila Weinberg. In 1964 she was, at the age of 18, the youngest detainee under the 90 Day detention law. Held for 55 days in solitary confinement, she went on hunger strike. Later she was imprisoned for six months for ANC activities. During the early seventies she was secretary of the Human Rights Committee in Johannesburg, and is now banned and under house-arrest in Johannesburg.

White women in the streets of
Johannesburg protest against apartheid.

Helen Joseph. Fifteen years under banning orders, detained in
1960 for several months, charged in the Treason Trial. This
photograph was taken when she was under house-arrest and not
permitted to go out beyond this gate at which she is standing. At
the age of seventy-three, she was sentenced to imprisonment
because she refused to testify against Winnie Mandela, wife of
Nelson Mandela, the ANC leader who is serving a life sentence on
Robben Island.

Florence Mkhize under house-arrest in Natal.

Esther Maleke with her son George. The photograph was taken in 1976, just before she was arrested, and sentenced to five years imprisonment.

The Federation of South African Women, together with the ANC Women's League, organised the legendary march of women to Pretoria on 9 August, 1956, when 20,000 of them, many with babies on their backs, assembled at Union Buildings, the seat of the regime, to present a petition to the Prime Minister against the extension of the pass system to women.

The Federation is not banned in South Africa, but its officials and many of its members are prevented from taking part in its work by restrictions, house-arrest and imprisonment.

At a conference of the Women's Federation in 1956. There was an exhibition: 'Women of all lands'.

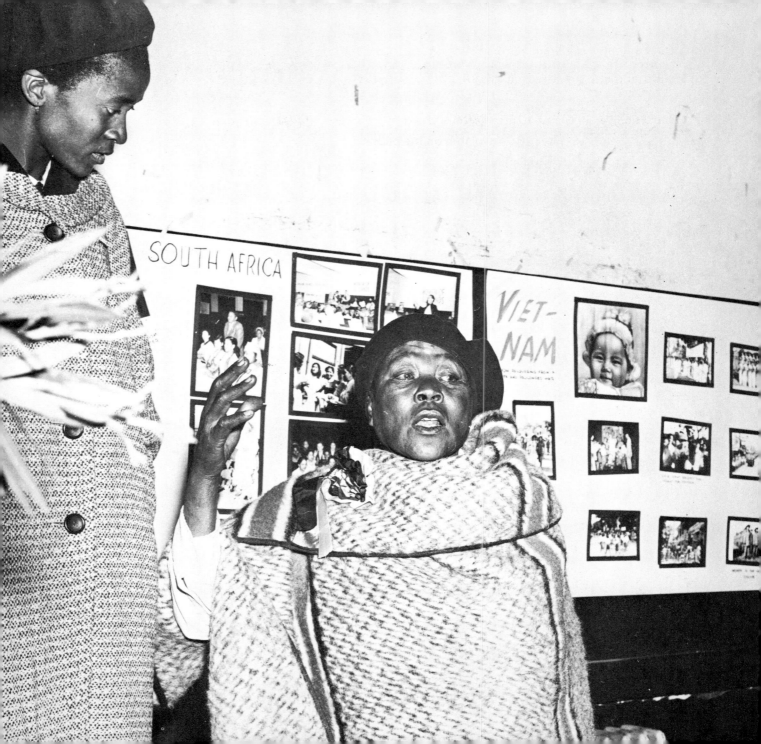

Children and Education

The fight against 'Bantu Education'

The Bantu Education Act was passed in 1953. It transferred education from the Education Department to the Bantu Affairs Department and placed the financial

burden for schooling on the parents. White education is free and compulsory up to the age of sixteen; there is nothing like that for black children. After the introduction of Bantu Education all African schools, including those run by churches and missions, and all private schools, had to comply with the Bantu Education syllabus or were deregistered. The Bantu Education syllabus is designed 'to fit the Bantu more effectively for their future occupations', namely to be unskilled labourers. An inferior type of education was being foisted on the people.

Growing up in a shantytown.

This lucky toddler is one of very few who has found a place in a creche financed by a handful of charitable and conscience stricken white women. This is no solution for the overwhelming majority of African mothers. The state does not provide any creches for African children, nor does it offer any subsidies.

The African National Congress organised the people to withdraw their children from the primary schools in protest against discriminatory education, but there was the grave problem of leaving the children in the streets. It was illegal to run independent schools and, in any case, this required funds beyond the ability of the Africans to raise. In many areas the ANC organised 'cultural clubs', which conducted education under cover of cultural activities, but this was patently illegal and the government forced these institutions to close down.

In the Germiston district a group of ANC parents and teachers started a school in an old tin church. This was the staff: from left to right: Bernard Molewa, Peggy Ras, Simon Makue (Principal), Angus Maphike, Pauline Makue.

Mother is at work; the young must look after the young.

At early morning exercise.

Classes in the improvised school were rather informal, but the children, conscious of the political implications, displayed a high degree of discipline and responsibility.

African students were excluded from the so-called 'open' universities by the perversely named Extension of University Education Act, which was introduced by the apartheid regime. The white students and teaching staff adopted a resolution of protest and proceeded to cover the main building of Witwatersrand University with the text.

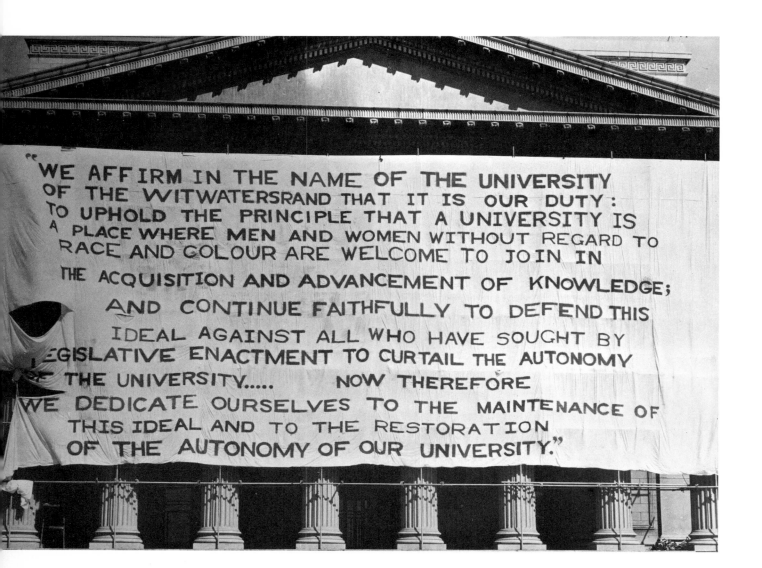

(overleaf) The principal reads a letter from the Bantu Affairs Department ordering the immediate closure of the school.

The struggle against Bantu Education is going on in South Africa and a new generation has taken it up in sharper form than ever before. But the young people also realise that the problem of education can only be solved on a lasting basis when power is effectively in the hands of the people.

This generation, photographed in Soweto in about 1960, took up the struggle against Bantu Education in a new and sharper form in June 1976.

Campaigns, Events and Solidarity

The end of the Coloured vote

In 1951, Dr. D. F. Malan, then Prime Minister, decided finally to abolish the voting rights of the Coloured people, which were entrenched in the constitution. The War Veterans' Action Committee, an organisation of white ex-service men with strong anti-fascist ideas, conducted a nationwide protest campaign of petitions and meetings which gained mass support. But the government rode roughshod even over the opposition of white voters. In a series of shady, and possibly illegal, moves the Coloured people were finally removed from the common voting roll.

The Rev. Douglas C. Thompson, a Methodist minister who was later banned and also held in prison, addresses a meeting of white voters at the City Hall in Johannesburg.

Collecting signatures to uphold the constitution.

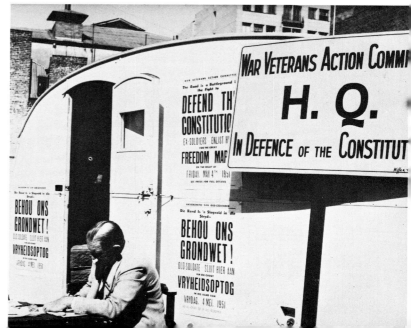

The Defiance Campaign

At its annual conference on 17 December 1951 the African National Congress decided to launch a campaign for the defiance of unjust laws. It was joined by the South African Indian Congress under the leadership of Dr. Y. M. Dadoo, its President. Following an inaugural meeting in Fordsburg, Johannesburg, on Freedom Day, 26 June 1952, eight thousand volunteers throughout the country proceeded to break apartheid laws. Africans entered through doors reserved for whites, whites entered townships of Africans without permits, Coloureds rode in trains marked 'Europeans Only' and Indians occupied white group areas. They were all arrested and jailed. The

Volunteers arrive at Fordsburg 'Freedom Square' for the opening of the Defiance Campaign, 26 June 1952.

The contingent of the South African Indian Congress, led by Dr. Y. M. Dadoo and Dr. G. M. Naicker.

The poster reads: 'Malan, remember how Hitler fell'. In the foreground, right, is Leslie Massina, later first Secretary of the South African Congress of Trade Unions.

Thousands were in attendance at the opening of the campaign.

The first to defy the unjust laws, Nelson Mandela (on the right) and Yusuf Dadoo, break their banning order by addressing a prohibited meeting. In this photograph they are about to surrender themselves to the police.

government introduced stringent regulations providing for whipping and long prison sentences for offences committed by way of protest. Meetings were prohibited, and more and more banning orders were served on individual opponents of apartheid.

19th Conference of the South African Indian Congress

In 1952, when the South African Indian Congress held its 19th conference in the Gandhi Hall, Johannesburg, the close alliance with the African National Congress was demonstrated by the presence of Dr. Moroka, then President of the ANC.

Opening session of the conference.

Dr. Y. M. Dadoo, President of the South African Indian Congress.

Public meeting in honour of the conference. Portraits of Dadoo and Moroka were symbolic of their close unity.

Human Rights Day

A mass demonstration by the African National Congress marked Human Rights Day, 10 December 1952, in Alexandra Township, Johannesburg. A procession culminated in a mass meeting.

The procession led by Walter Sisulu, General Secretary of the ANC.

Ruth First; the interpreter is John Mavuso, an ANC activist.

On the platform at the meeting: Yusuf Cachalia of the SA Indian Congress, Walter Sisulu, Ruth First, Albertina Sisulu. Walter Sisulu is serving a life sentence on Robben Island; his wife Albertina is banned and restricted to a small suburb of Soweto; Ruth First is in exile.

Walter Sisulu addresses the
meeting.

The huge audience
enthusiastically votes for
human rights.

Mass meetings protesting against the removals.

Western Areas Removals

In 1953 the government issued orders to the residents of Sophiatown and Western Native Townships of Johannesburg to move. Many Africans had title deeds to land and property in Sophiatown and adjoining areas, but the government was intent on turning them into landless workers. The racists also objected to the presence of blacks in proximity to such white residential areas as Newclare and Westdene. The African National Congress called on the people to resist the move. Anti-removal meetings were held and thousands attended but, despite popular opposition, the government enforced the removal by mobilising an overwhelming force of 2,000 police, reinforced by army units, including armoured vehicles—a military operation of major dimensions.

On the morning of the forcible removal of hundreds of families. The Reverend Trevor Huddleston, in the company of Ida Mntwana (ANC women's leader) and Robert Resha (in centre, with black coat, the leader of the Anti-Removal Campaign) had been touring the township, but were unable to stop the removals.

The banning of Chief Albert Luthuli

On 11 July 1954 the African National Congress organised a meeting in Sophiatown, which was to have been addressed by the ANC President, Chief Albert Luthuli. However, when he arrived at the airport in Johannesburg, Chief Luthuli was served with a banning order, prohibiting him from attending gatherings and restricting him to the village of Groutville in Natal. He was forced to return to Natal, but the meeting proceeded in his absence, attended by over 10,000 people.

Chief Albert Luthuli.

Walter Sisulu reads Luthuli's speech. In the centre foreground is my little daughter Sheila, my wife Violet and Helen Joseph, later the first woman to be placed under house-arrest.

This meeting had some consequence for me. I was prohibited from attending gatherings in terms of an extensive banning order. After this meeting I was charged with breaking my order. Police agents gave evidence that I had moved about in the crowd with a camera suspended from my neck. In my defence I produced my camera, a heavy hand-held Linhof, as well as the photographs taken by me on that occasion, showing that I had been on a roof some 50 yards away from the meeting. The prints and the negatives became part of the court record. At the end of the trial the magistrate rejected the police evidence and I was acquitted. Later when I applied for the return of my negatives I found to my horror that the clerks had punched holes in them for filing purposes! Fortunately, in a few cases these holes were in strategically unimportant places, as in the roof in photo above.

At another meeting which Chief Luthuli was prevented from attending, his presence was marked by a huge portrait. The thugs of the security police threw a bottle of purple ink over the picture.

National Day of Protest

26 June has been marked in South Africa ever since 1950 as a national day of protest and has become known as Freedom Day. In 1957 the ANC organised a protest march on that day, which culminated in a massive meeting outside the City Hall in Johannesburg. The hall itself is barred to Africans, but the Mayor, Councillor Max Goodman, consented to receive a deputation.

The procession reaches the City Hall.

Stay-at-home, 14 – 16 April 1958

The African National Congress called for a stay-at-home on the occasion of the general election which, of course, involved whites only. How does one photograph a stay-at-home? I went out to one of the townships at three o'clock in the morning, the time when workers begin to line up at the buses to go to work. Usually the buses were overcrowded and people were often late for work, unless they got to the buses early. However, that morning the streets were empty and silent. Then suddenly truckloads of police arrived and arranged themselves at various strategic points. Gradually, the people came out into the streets and watched with some amusement the nervous antics of the police. But nobody mounted the buses. The policemen became edgy and irritable and finally let their anger out at known ANC officials who were mingling with the crowd.

Police on duty during stay-at-home.

The demonstrators, estimated at over 20,000, crowded the streets and the front of the City Hall. White officials complained that their flower beds had been trampled.

People mill around, watching.

The buses wait, surrounded by police, but nobody mounts them. (overleaf).

The police stop Peter Nthite, ANC Youth leader, and Jonas Matlou, and begin to frisk them. The irony of the 'Hands Off' sign left from a previous campaign is lost on the servants of the law.

The police order Peter and Jonas into Peter's own car and make them drive to the police station, where they are detained, to be released later without a charge.

Matlou remonstrates with the policeman, because there is no warrant to search and the police action is illegal.

The Pondoland troubles

Protests and unrest were not restricted to the urban areas. In the late 1950s the whole countryside was seething with discontent, from the Transkei to the Orange Free State, from the Western Transvaal to Natal. Everywhere there were clashes with the authorities.

Pondoland is a part of what is now the Transkei bantustan. Interference with the tribesmen's traditional grazing rights, arbitrary dismissals and appointments of tribal chiefs, imposition of unpopular 'Bantu Authorities', disputes with government appointed headmen and village management boards — all this led to severe unrest and troubles. The tribesmen elected their own authorities, which became known as 'The Mountain'. This clandestine authority conducted secret trials of traitors and government appointees and inflicted severe punishments.

Tribesmen gather for a meeting to present their grievances to government officials.

Leaders of the tribesmen from left to right: M. Mtshangase, H. Mbodla, T. Tshangela, S. Madikizela, S. M. Pini.

The minions of apartheid: Victor Leibbrandt, Bantu Commissioner and magistrate at Bizana; T. van Heerden, Bantu Commissioner at Lusikisiki. The third man is a security policeman.

The tribesmen listen patiently to the proceedings.

S. Madikizela acts as spokesman.

Eventually the South African government, unable to exert its authority by normal methods, imposed a State of Emergency over the entire area. This has remained in operation to this day, a quarter of a century later. Kaiser Matanzima, the notorious stooge tribal chief of the Transkei bantustan, has taken over the emergency decrees which he inherited from his white racist masters and continues to enforce them. The photographs illustrate one of the numerous confrontations between the tribesmen and the authorities in 1954.

Kaiser Matanzima—government by force.

The Congress of the People and the Freedom Charter

The initial proposal to convene a Congress of the People came from Professor Z. K. Mathews in his presidential address to the Cape Province conference of the African National Congress on 15 August 1953. The final decision was taken at the annual conference of the ANC in December 1953 and Chief Luthuli, as President, issued a 'Call' in May 1954, published in several languages and widely distributed throughout the country by 10,000 'freedom volunteers' for whom a distinctive uniform had been designed. These volunteers canvassed people in every part of the country, and collected demands from representative groups and organisations at numerous meetings. Eventually, all these demands were collated and formulated in the Freedom Charter.

Professor Z. K. Matthews.

The Freedom Charter

We, the People of South Africa, declare for all our country and the world to know:

that South Africa belongs to all who live in it, black and white, and that no government can justly claim authority unless it is based on the will of all the people;

that our people have been robbed of their birthright to land, liberty and peace by a form of government founded on injustice and inequality;

that our country will never be prosperous or free until all our people live in brotherhood, enjoying equal rights and opportunities;

that only a democratic state, based on the will of all the people, can secure to all their birthright without distinction of colour, race, sex or belief;

And therefore, we, the people of South Africa, black and white together—equals, countrymen and brothers—adopt this Freedom Charter. And we pledge ourselves to strive together, sparing neither strength nor courage, until the democratic changes here set out have been won.

THE PEOPLE SHALL GOVERN!

Every man and woman shall have the right to vote for and to stand as a candidate for all bodies which make laws;

All people shall be entitled to take part in the administration of the country;

The rights of the people shall be the same, regardless of race, colour or sex;

All bodies of minority rule, advisory boards, councils and authorities shall be replaced by democratic organs of self-government.

ALL NATIONAL GROUPS SHALL HAVE EQUAL RIGHTS!

There shall be equal status in the bodies of state, in the courts and in the schools for all national groups and races;

All people shall have equal right to use their own languages, and to develop their own folk culture and customs;

All national groups shall be protected by law against insults to their race and national pride;

The preaching and practice of national, race or colour discrimination and contempt shall be a punishable crime;

All apartheid laws and practices shall be set aside.

THE PEOPLE SHALL SHARE IN THE COUNTRY'S WEALTH!

The national wealth of our country, the heritage of all South Africans, shall be restored to the people;

The mineral wealth beneath the soil, the banks and monopoly industry shall be transferred to the ownership of the people as a whole;
All other industry and trade shall be controlled to assist the well-being of the people;
All people shall have equal rights to trade where they choose, to manufacture and to enter all trades, crafts and professions.

THE LAND SHALL BE SHARED AMONG THOSE WHO WORK IT!
Restrictions of land ownership on a racial basis shall be ended, and all the land redivided amongst those who work it, to banish famine and land hunger;
The state shall help the peasants with implements, seed, tractors and dams to save the soil and assist the tillers;
Freedom of movement shall be guaranteed to all who work on the land;
All shall have the right to occupy land wherever they choose;
People shall not be robbed of their cattle, and forced labour and farm prisons shall be abolished.

ALL SHALL BE EQUAL BEFORE THE LAW!
No one shall be imprisoned, deported or restricted without a fair trial;
No one shall be condemned by the order of any Government official;
The courts shall be representative of all the people;
Imprisonment shall be only for serious crimes against the people, and shall aim at re-education, not vengeance;
The police force and army shall be open to all on an equal basis and shall be the helpers and protectors of the people;
All laws which discriminate on grounds of race, colour or belief shall be repealed.

ALL SHALL ENJOY EQUAL HUMAN RIGHTS!
The law shall guarantee to all their right to speak, to organise, to meet together, to publish, to preach, to worship and to educate their children;
The privacy of the house from police raids shall be protected by law;
All shall be free to travel without restriction from countryside to town, from province to province, and from South Africa abroad;
Pass Laws, permits and all other laws restricting these freedoms shall be abolished.

THERE SHALL BE WORK AND SECURITY!
All who work shall be free to form trade unions, to elect their officers and to make wage agreements with their employers;
The state shall recognise the right and duty of all to work, and to draw full unemployment benefits;
Men and women of all races shall receive equal pay for equal work;
There shall be a forty-hour working week, a national minimum wage, paid annual leave, and sick leave for all workers, and maternity leave on full pay for all working mothers;
Miners, domestic workers, farm workers and civil servants shall have the same rights as all others who work;
Child labour, compound labour, the tot system and contract labour shall be abolished.

THE DOORS OF LEARNING AND OF CULTURE SHALL BE OPENED!

The government shall discover, develop and encourage national talent for the enhancement of our cultural life;

All the cultural treasures of mankind shall be open to all, by free exchange of books, ideas and contact with other lands;

The aim of education shall be to teach the youth to love their people and their culture, to honour human brotherhood, liberty and peace;

Education shall be free, compulsory, universal and equal for all children;

Higher education and technical training shall be opened to all by means of state allowances and scholarships awarded on the basis of merit;

Adult illiteracy shall be ended by a mass state education plan;

Teachers shall have all the rights of other citizens;

The colour bar in cultural life, in sport and in education shall be abolished.

THERE SHALL BE HOUSES, SECURITY AND COMFORT!

All people shall have the right to live where they choose, to be decently housed, and to bring up their families in comfort and security;

Unused housing space to be made available to the people;

Rent and prices shall be lowered, food plentiful and no one shall go hungry;

A preventive health scheme shall be run by the state;

Free medical care and hospitalisation shall be provided for all, with special care for mothers and young children;

Slums shall be demolished, and new suburbs built where all have transport, roads, lighting, playing fields, creches and social centres;

The aged, the orphans, the disabled and the sick shall be cared for by the state;

Rest, leisure and recreation shall be the right of all;

Fenced locations and ghettoes shall be abolished, and laws which break up families shall be repealed.

THERE SHALL BE PEACE AND FRIENDSHIP!

South Africa shall be a fully independent state, which respects the rights and sovereignty of all nations;

South Africa shall strive to maintain world peace and the settlement of all international disputes by negotiation—not war;

Peace and friendship amongst all our people shall be secured by upholding the equal rights, opportunities and status of all;

The people of the protectorates—Basutoland, Bechuanaland and Swaziland shall be free to decide for themselves their own future;

The right of all the peoples of Africa to independence and self-government shall be recognised, and shall be the basis of close co-operation.

Let all who love their people and their country now say, as we say here: "THESE FREEDOMS WE WILL FIGHT FOR, SIDE BY SIDE, THROUGHOUT OUR LIVES, UNTIL WE HAVE WON OUR LIBERTY."

The uniform of the 'Freedom Volunteers'.

The preparations for the Congress were planned by the 'Congress Alliance', headed by the African National Congress. Other members of the Alliance were the South African Indian Congress, the South African Congress of Trade Unions, the Coloured People's Congress and the Congress of Democrats (an organisation of white supporters of the ANC). An emblem was designed to symbolise this Alliance, consisting of a wheel representing the ANC and four spokes for the other parties.

Canvassing for the Congress of the People.

A welcoming committee for the delegates.

The Congress of the People met on 25 and 26 June 1955 on an open square in Kliptown, near Johannesburg. It was a prodigious job of organisation and popular endeavour. Transport for some 3,000 people had to be arranged, they had to be accommodated and fed for two days. Even toilet facilities had to be specially planned. Many delegates never reached the Congress, as the police had erected road blocks in many parts of the country and detained some 200 delegates. Nevertheless, when the Congress opened, there were 2,884 accredited delegates present, of whom 320 were Indians, 230 Coloureds and 112 whites. In addition there were about 3,000 observers who watched the proceedings from behind a canvas enclosure set up to separate the public from the official delegates.

Early arrivals including Kate Molale.

A delegation from a women's organisation.

Delegates from the Transkei.

A group of Indian women, headed by Dr. Y. M. Dadoo's aged mother.

The catering department had to make provision for delegates who were vegetarians. Accordingly they prepared different soups. At the subsequent Treason Trial the prosecution produced amongst the thousands of exhibits various signs reading: 'Soup with meat' and 'Soup without meat' — presumably as evidence of high treason!

Various delegations parade with their demands.

Freedom
OF
Speech
REMOVAL
OF
We want
Better
houses
Free
Education
Pay

WESTERN NATIVE TOWNSHIP
THERE SHALL BE WORK AND SECURITY
ALL SHALL ENJOY EQUAL HUMAN RIGHTS
AFRICA MAYIBUYE

A delegation from one of the rural areas.

A delegation from Natal.

On the platform during one of the sessions.

The Congress of the People in session.

A view of the Congress from the 'public gallery'.

As usual I had to resort to subterfuge to photograph the Congress. I was banned from attending gatherings, so I had arranged for myself a grandstand view from a nearby roof, where I set up my equipment. Two other photographers were working under my direction amongst the crowd. I found to my dismay that my vantage point attracted other members of the public who clambered up on the same roof and settled down right in front of where I was working. This also attracted the attention of the security police, then known as the Special Branch, who were swarming about everywhere. An angry Colonel Spengler, head of the Special Branch, came storming up to me: 'Weinberg, if you don't bugger off this minute, I will arrest you and charge you with attending a gathering!' I had no alternative but to 'bugger off', but actually this proved to be fortunate, as shortly afterwards armed police surrounded the Congress, searched and took the names of everybody present and confiscated documents, papers, leaflets and even films. By that time I was already ensconced in my darkroom developing the photographs for delivery for the next edition of *New Age*.

A view of the platform.

At the first session, the 'Isitwalandwe' medal was presented to Chief Albert Luthuli, Dr. Y. M. Dadoo and Father Trevor Huddleston for distinguished service in the struggle for freedom. Only Trevor Huddleston was there to receive the medal. The other two were banned.

Ida Mntwana leads the Congress in a freedom song.

Despite police interference, the Congress adopted the Freedom Charter, and afterwards, on 31 March 1956, a Special Conference of the African National Congress adopted it as its official programme.

The Treason Trial—the main attack on the Freedom Charter

Throughout 1955 and 1956 the Special Branch conducted a series of raids on offices and private homes of hundreds of opponents of apartheid. Documents, letters, pamphlets, even pieces of clothing were seized in preparation for a show trial. Finally, early on the morning of 5 December 1956, hundreds of policemen throughout the country descended on the homes of leaders of the Congress Alliance and arrested them. One hundred and fifty-six people—104 Africans, 23 Whites, 21 Indians and 8 Coloureds—were charged with high treason, a capital offence in South Africa. While the case was remanded against most of the accused, 30 of them sat in court almost daily for four-and-a-half years, their normal lives disrupted, and had to listen to an endless recital of long documents, garbled reports of ANC meetings and fabrications by bought informers. Outside, the struggle of the people was continuing in the streets, the bus-boycott ran its bitter but successful course, there were pass burnings, there were stay-at-homes and there was the State of Emergency when the government showed itself unable to continue with 'normal' methods of administration. The Treason Trial was the main attack on the Freedom Charter, but in the end the court acquitted and discharged all the accused.

A group photograph of all the accused. The story of this photograph illustrates an aspect of racism in South Africa. I had spoken to the superintendent of Joubert Park (in the vicinity of the court) and had asked for permission to use an amphitheatrical seating arrangement in the park for the purpose of a group photograph of 156 people. He readily agreed. About half-an-hour before the time appointed to take the photograph (during the court lunch break) I went there again for a final check-up and on this occasion he asked: 'By the way, who are these people whom you are photographing'? When I told him, he threw his hands up in horror. 'You are not going to bring all these "kaffirs" into Joubert Park!' and promptly withdrew permission. Within the half-hour left to the lunch break of the court I hastily improvised. I borrowed some benches and photographed the accused seated in groups of 35 or 40 in the same alphabetical and provincial order as in the court and then prepared a montage of the resulting four groups.

The ACCUSED

DECEMBER 1956

On the day the Treason Trial opened, the streets outside the court were thronged with thousands of demonstrators. Traffic had to be diverted. At one time the police became panicky and some wild shots were fired off. But the demonstrators remained disciplined and their sympathy with the accused was undisguised as they lined up behind posters with the slogan 'We stand by our leaders'.

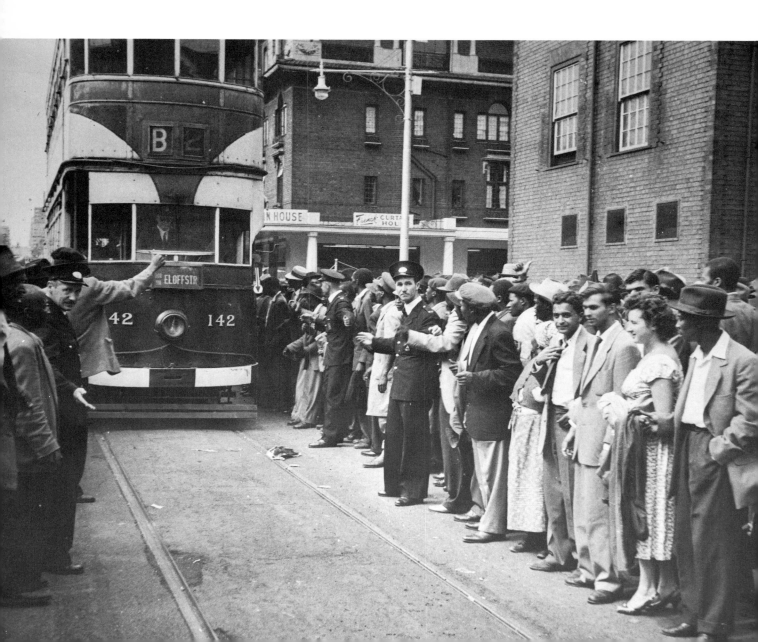

The prison vans loaded with the accused were greeted with the ANC thumbs up sign, to which the accused responded with equal enthusiasm through the bars of the vans.

Running the gauntlet of Special Branch detectives and police, one of the defence lawyers, Vernon Berrangè (with stick), arrives. In the background are Dr. Yusuf Dadoo and Goolam Pahad, leaders of the SA Indian Congress.

Three of the women accused get out of the prison van, Sonia Bunting, Yettah Barenblatt and Helen Joseph.
The police photographer and a detective discover my presence upstairs.

I manage to catch a shot of M. P. Naicker (he later became editor of *Sechaba,* the official organ of the ANC, and died in exile) and a group of white accused, when the Special Branch detective (bottom of photo over page) ordered me out.

Bram Fischer (on the right) was one of the leading lawyers in the Treason Trial. On the left is his father who was Judge President of the Orange Free State. Almost a decade later Bram Fischer was himself arrested and sentenced to life imprisonment. Bram died in jail in 1975 and the prison authorities refused to hand over his ashes to his family.

Moretseli's restaurant

An interesting sidelight on the Treason Trial: E. P. Moretseli, one of the accused who was chairman of the Transvaal Region of the ANC, had a restaurant which was popularly known as 'Retsies'. Many treason trialists used to gather there during the court lunch breaks. Retsie must have supplied more lunches free during the trial than he ever sold during the years that his restaurant existed. 'Old Retsie' is dead now, but everybody in the ANC will remember him with warm affection.

'Old Retsie' discusses the problems of the day with some members of the ANC.

At 'Retsies'. Note the *New Age* poster on the wall.

The Central Indian High School in Fordsburg

The Indian people living in Fordsburg, Vrededorp and adjoining suburbs in Johannesburg were ordered to move in terms of the Group Areas Act. A ghetto had been established for them in Lenasia, 20 miles away. For a long time the Indian people resisted this incursion on their rights. Then the government attempted to coerce them by closing down the schools and trying to force the children to make the long daily ride to Lenasia and back. Under the leadership of the South African Indian Congress, a Parents Association was formed, which established a private high school in Fordsburg and managed to run it for a time. The Group Areas Act is a part of the degrading and humiliating system of apartheid.

The office of the Indian Parents' Association was situated in Ferreira Street, where the African National Congress also had its premises.

The staff of the Central Indian High School: Thandray (vice-principal), Alfred Hutchinson (a well known writer who died in exile), Molly Fischer (wife of Bram Fischer), Duma Nokwe, Michael Harmel (principal), P. Anderson and M. Moosajee.

Morning assembly. Many of these children have since played an active role in the liberation movement.

The Bus Boycott

During 1956 and early 1957 the main transport company on the Witwatersrand, the Putco Bus Company, announced increases in fares of one penny on a four penny ride. To the people this attack on their miserably inadequate incomes was intolerable and it was decided to boycott the buses. 'Azikwelwa' (they shall not be ridden!) became the cry all along the Witwatersrand, in Alexandra, Sophiatown and Randfontein, and in Pretoria as well. For many months people walked to work, and back, every day. For the people of Alexandra it meant a daily march into Johannesburg and back of ten miles each way. They set out in the mornings long before sunrise and came home at night after dark. Many bought or borrowed bicycles, some used taxis, but nobody rode the buses.

Women march, many with heavy bundles on their heads.

Four o'clock in the morning: boycotters set out for the ten mile walk to work.

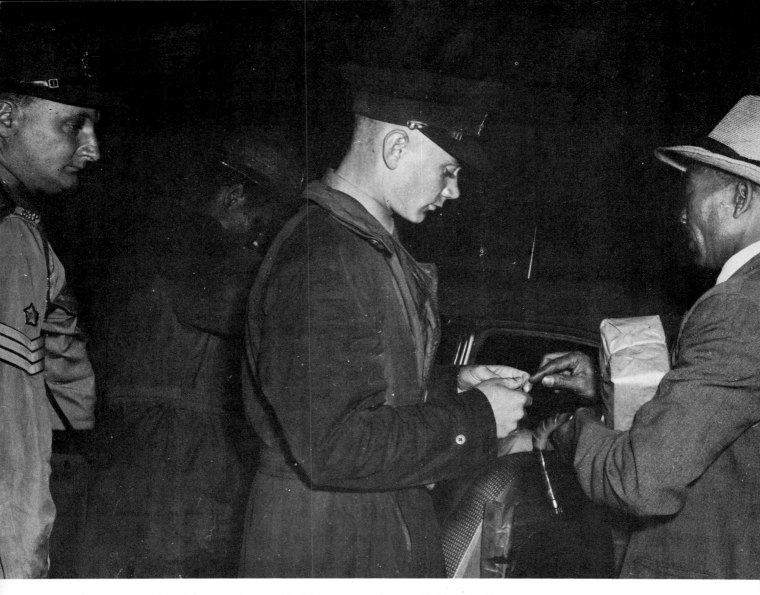

This man was forced out of the car of a friendly white driver who was giving him a lift. The white driver was threatened with prosecution.

The government tried to break the boycott by police harrassment and intimidation. One ANC youth, Joel Ramosodi of Pretoria, was shot dead by the police. Every day, on the long line of march, policemen stopped and harrassed men and women, asking for passes, pawing through their belongings, generally behaving in an arrogant and provocative manner. When sympathetic whites offered the marchers lifts in their motorcars, the police prosecuted them for carrying passengers without licences. But the people would be neither provoked nor intimidated and they continued to walk. The employers became apprehensive when the boycotters threatened that they would stop walking to work and would stay at home. After many months, Putco dropped the proposed increase in fares. Employers agreed to pay a transport levy and the government undertook to subsidise Putco.

Women are harassed and their parcels and belongings searched. White children look on bewildered, whilst the women proceed stoically on their long and weary way.

The police line the streets in an effort to intimidate; they check passes, they threaten, but the people walk on proudly.

A funeral becomes a mass demonstration

Ida Mntwana, a venerated ANC woman leader died during the Treason Trial. Meetings and demonstrations of the ANC were banned at the time, but the ANC decided to make Ida's funeral an occasion for the defiance of the law. Thousands of men and women followed the hearse, bearing the colours and wearing the uniforms of the ANC.

Hundreds line the streets of Western Native Township, Ida Mntwana's home, and the hearse is followed by a long cortege of cars and buses carrying mourners.

Defiantly men and women display ANC banners and uniforms.

A guard of honour at the entrance to the cemetery.

Lilian Ngoyi gives the funeral oration.

Mourners around the grave-side.

The coffin is carried by leaders of the ANC Women's League, amongst them Albertina Sisulu, Winnie Mandela, Viola Hashe.

The coffin covered with an ANC flag, is lowered into the grave.

Pass burning

Just before the ANC was declared an illegal organisation in 1960, there was a defiant campaign of pass burning. Chief Luthuli gave the signal by burning his own pass.

Duma Nokwe and Dr. A. Letele follow the example of the President of the ANC.

Pass after Pass is thrown upon the fire.

The flames consume the hated pass books.

The whole township population gives the ANC thumbs up salute, the sign of African unity.   (over page).

The struggle continues

After the ANC was banned, the government had hoped that popular resistance would subside. But the struggle continued underground. The slogans of the ANC appeared regularly in the streets of Johannesburg and other cities; leaflets and publications of the banned organisation circulated widely. There were trials and imprisonments, but the evidence was there that the ANC was very much alive and that the people were rallying to its call for armed resistance. Courageous underground activists were continuing to mobilise and organise the people.

Slogan on the wall of a bank.

On the Johannesburg Public Library, from which blacks are barred.

In a busy thoroughfare where buses pass daily taking people to and from work.

In a white suburb.

The signwriter took his time about this slogan.

On a wall surrounding a government establishment. (over page).

What of the Future?

The youth come again to the fore

Soweto was no accident. It grew out of the past which is described, somewhat inadequately, in these photographs. Hundreds of young people, aroused by their own bitter experiences, are joining the African National Congress. Many are already playing an active and leading part in the struggle.

In the late 1940s the ANC experienced the revitalising influence of members of its Youth League, who were emerging with new ideas, with burning enthusiasm and with dedication born out of their knowledge that freedom can only be achieved by sacrifice and struggle. These were men like Nelson Mandela, Walter Sisulu, Govan Mbeki and others, many of whom are now serving life sentences on Robben Island. Today the young are again coming to the fore, taking their place in the march which was begun long ago when the ANC was formed in 1912.

Chief Luthuli who was awarded the Nobel Peace Prize, said:

'. . . who will deny that thirty years of my life have been spent knocking in vain, patiently, moderately and modestly at a closed and barred door? What have been the fruits of moderation? The past thirty years have seen the greatest number of laws restricting our rights and progress, until today we have reached a stage where we have no rights at all.'

In one of his memorable addresses as President of the Transvaal ANC, Nelson Mandela took this further:

'. . . the old methods of bringing about mass actions through public mass meetings, press statements and leaflets . . . have become difficult to use effectively . . . (we) require the development of new forms of struggle . . . on a higher level . . . there is no easy walk to freedom anywhere . . .'

And the Manifesto of Umkhonto we Sizwe, issued on 16 December 1961, drew the logical conclusion:

'The time comes in the life of any nation when there remain only two choices — submit or fight. That time has now come to South Africa. We shall not submit and we have no choice but to hit back by all means in our power in defence of our people, our future and our freedom.'

Nelson Mandela.

Soweto students, who left the country to join the external mission of the ANC in search of education, training and political guidance, lead an anti-apartheid march through the streets of Dar es Salaam in Tanzania.

LA VIJANA WA TANU
RETRIBUTION for the DEATHS of OUR
LONG LIVE THE
NO ARMS FOR APARTHEID SOUTH AFRICA
WE DEMAND TRADE UNION RIGHTS IN SOUTH AFRICA
WE MOURN SOWETO
THOUSANDS IN JAILS
HUNDRENDS WOUNDED